TRAINING MANAGERS TO TRAIN
A Practical Guide
To Improving Employee Performance

by Brother Herman E. Zaccarelli, C.S.C.

A FIFTY-MINUTE™ SERIES BOOK

CRISP PUBLICATIONS, INC.
Menlo Park, California

TRAINING MANAGERS TO TRAIN

A Practical Guide To Improving Employee Performance

Brother Herman E. Zaccarelli, C.S.C.

CREDITS
Editor: **Michael Crisp**
Designer: **Carol Harris**
Typesetting: **Interface Studio**
Cover Design: **Carol Harris**
Artwork: **Ralph Mapson**

Copyright © 1988 by Brother Herman E. Zaccarelli, C.S.C.
Printed in the United States of America

English language Crisp books are distributed worldwide. Our major international distributors include:

CANADA: Reid Publishing Ltd., Box 69559—109 Thomas St., Oakville, Ontario, Canada L6J 7R4. TEL: (905) 842-4428, FAX: (905) 842-9327

Raincoast Books Distribution Ltd., 112 East 3rd Avenue, Vancouver, British Columbia, Canada V5T 1C8. TEL: (604) 873-6581, FAX: (604) 874-2711

AUSTRALIA: Career Builders, P.O. Box 1051, Springwood, Brisbane, Queensland, Australia 4127. TEL: 841-1061, FAX: 841-1580

NEW ZEALAND: Career Builders, P.O. Box 571, Manurewa, Auckland, New Zealand. TEL: 266-5276, FAX: 266-4152

JAPAN: Phoenix Associates Co., Mizuho Bldg. 2-12-2, Kami Osaki, Shinagawa-Ku, Tokyo 141, Japan. TEL: 3-443-7231, FAX: 3-443-7640

Selected Crisp titles are also available in other languages. Contact International Rights Manager Suzanne Kelly at (415) 323-6100 for more information.

Library of Congress Catalog Card Number 87-73183
Zaccarelli, Herman E.
Training Managers To Train
ISBN 0-931961-43-2

This book is printed on recyclable paper with soy ink.

PREFACE

Managers at all organizational levels, whether they own their own business or work for someone else, must supervise people. Done correctly, everyone benefits and the manager will receive credit for a job well done. If, on the other hand, employees are not managed effectively, no one will benefit, and the manager will quickly get the blame! The task of directing people at work is not easy because employees, as human beings, are very complex. However, employees cannot perform well on the job no matter how hard they try and regardless of how much they want to until they know *what* they are supposed to do and *how* they are supposed to do it. A well-developed training program addresses both of these issues.

TRAINING MANAGERS TO TRAIN focuses on answering the question: How *exactly* does a manager prepare for, plan, present, and follow up on training programs designed to yield competent employees? The answer to this question is presented in the pages which follow.

Training programs can be fun to develop and to present. And they can make a significant difference in your organization's success. Readers will find this book easy to read and use. The efforts spent learning about training by putting the basic principles in this book to work can be rewarding to everyone—management, employees, and customers.

We're excited to bring this material to you. We hope you enjoy using it. Turn the page and let's get started!

ABOUT THIS BOOK

Why will learning from this book be interesting and fun? Because you are not going to just read it; you are going to use it! You'll be working with a pencil or pen as much as you'll be reading. In the process, you'll learn more because there will be opportunities to apply what you are learning.

This program is designed for you if:

—You are aspiring to become a manager and want to learn more about the many requirements of managing.

—You are already a manager and want to learn more about training.

—You are a trainer and want to get some ideas about programs which can be used to help other people learn how to train.

—You are a student and want to learn more about the instructional design aspects of training.

In addition to using this book as you work through it, you will also be able to use it later. If you encounter a problem that can be addressed through training once you are back on-the-job, this book will provide a review of techniques which will help you develop and implement training programs.

This book is part of the "FIFTY-MINUTE" SERIES. This implies you can work your way through it in one session. You will probably find it helpful to follow up your initial activity with a more detailed study of selected parts as you actually develop training programs. In effect, then, this book is a "recipe" to show you, in a step-by-step manner, how to train.

DEDICATION

This book is dedicated to:

Dr. and Mrs. Lewis J. Minor

and

George and Toodie St. Laurent

We read in our daily newspaper about business executives who take advantage of their positions to exploit others.

At the same time, there are exceptional entrepreneurs with high ethical standards and successful businesses. These individuals rarely make news but their quality of life is an inspiration to the business community.

Dr. and Mrs. Lewis Minor and George and Toodie St. Laurent are such people. They inspired me to "take the less traveled road" and because of the standards they set, my service to humankind has been richly blessed.

Brother Herman E. Zaccarelli, C.S.C.

CONTENTS

IT ALL STARTS WITH TRAINING OBJECTIVES

An objective states the purpose of the training; it tells what the trainer wants to accomplish. A *competency-based* objective tells the purpose from the trainee's perspective. It indicates what the trainee is expected to know or be able to do *after* the training is completed.

This guide is a training manual whose objectives can be stated in a competency format as shown on the facing page.

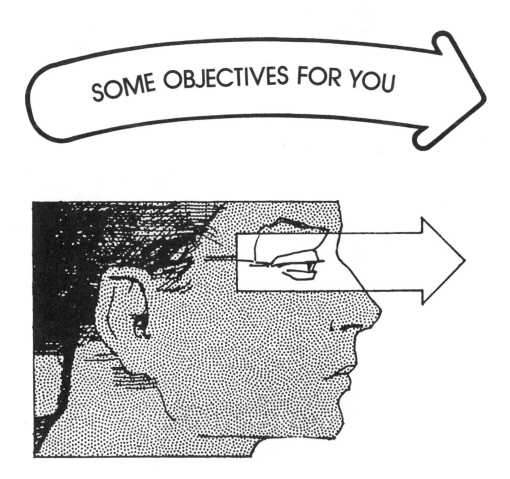

SOME OBJECTIVES FOR YOU

OBJECTIVES OF
TRAINING MANAGERS TO TRAIN

After reading this book and working through suggested exercises the reader will be able to master the following objectives: (Numbers refer to pages where the objective is discussed.)

Objectives	Page(s)
1. *Define* a competency-based trainee objective.	vi
2. *Know* why training is important from the perspective of both the trainer *and* the trainee.	3-7
3. *Give* a brief overview of the four basic steps in training program development and implementation.	14
4. *Conduct* a Position Analysis including the development of required analysis forms.	17-27
5. *Tell* four uses of a Job Description.	26
6. *Develop* training objectives, training plans, and training lessons.	30-35
7. *Select* qualified trainers.	37
8. *List* eight factors to weigh when considering group or individual training.	39
9. *Describe* major principles of group training.	40
10. *Design* an on-the-job training program which incorporates principles in the four-step method.	44-51
11. *Relate* training evaluation to the training program objectives.	52-53
12. *Recite* ten principles of coaching.	55
13. *Design* an orientation checklist.	59
14. *Consider* the role of employees in training program development and implementation.	60-61
15. *Know* where to locate helpful training resources.	63
16. *Use* visual aids/equipment effectively.	64-65

REASONS WHY TRAINING IS IMPORTANT

A manager is busy and has many things to do. There's only time for the most important, highest priority activities.

TRAINING STYLES

Every manager brings a different personality to training. This individual style, however, must be blended into an effective training format if the outcome is to be successful. Several reasons why training is important regardless of the trainer's style are described on the next page. Check ☑ those with which you agree.

REASONS WHY TRAINING IS IMPORTANT

Which of the following would benefit your organization?

☐ **Saving Money**—If employees know how to do work the *right* way, costs will be lower; profits will be higher.

☐ **Saving Employees**—Employees who know how to do work according to their boss's expectations will be less anxious and turnover will be reduced.

☐ **Saving Customers and Making New Ones**—Customers are happy when they receive the products/services they expect. Training helps assure that this will *consistently* happen.

We hope you checked *all* of the above. Training can provide all of these benefits. You, your customers, your employees, and your organization have much to gain—and nothing to lose—with a high quality training program. Which of the following will benefit your organization?

☐ **Saving Time**—A trained staff will promote efficiency. Both the manager's time and that of employees will be saved.

☐ **Reducing Staffing Concerns**—Trained employees are better prepared and more eligible for promotion opportunities.

☐ **Saving Relationships**—Managers who show their concern for employees with quality training help motivate them and morale levels are likely to increase.

Give yourself an "A" if you checked all six boxes.

TRAINING IS PART OF EFFECTIVE SUPERVISION

A manager must do many things at once. All are important. Nothing is *more* important than training.

The management of people determines organizational success. Training cannot wait until "the manager gets around to it" or "when time permits."

Training must receive a high priority from management. The highest levels of management must agree about the importance of training and allocate time and resources for it to be done well.

No manager can train in a vacuum. Top management must endorse the value of training and employees must be convinced of what training will do for them.

MANAGERS MUST BE EFFECTIVE TRAINERS

TRAINING KNOW HOW IS A MUST FOR MANAGERS

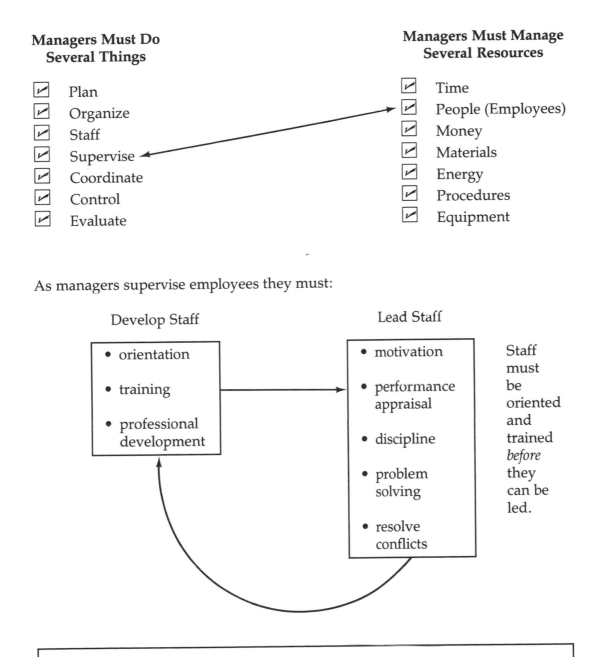

Managers Must Do Several Things

☑ Plan
☑ Organize
☑ Staff
☑ Supervise
☑ Coordinate
☑ Control
☑ Evaluate

Managers Must Manage Several Resources

☑ Time
☑ People (Employees)
☑ Money
☑ Materials
☑ Energy
☑ Procedures
☑ Equipment

As managers supervise employees they must:

Develop Staff

- orientation
- training
- professional development

Lead Staff

- motivation
- performance appraisal
- discipline
- problem solving
- resolve conflicts

Staff must be oriented and trained *before* they can be led.

TRAINING IS NOT A LUXURY FOR MANAGERS...IT IS A NECESSITY!

EMPLOYEES BENEFIT FROM TRAINING

Employees benefit from training. Management's job is to demonstrate how training will help employees. Properly explained, employees will *want* to be trained. They will *participate* in training activities. They will receive *maximum* benefits from their training experience.

WHAT DO EMPLOYEES GET OUT OF TRAINING?

There's an old saying, "If a trainee hasn't learned it's because the trainer hasn't trained." Trainees who understand the benefits they will receive from training will want to learn.

EMPLOYEES BENEFIT FROM TRAINING (Continued)

Check any of the following you would like to achieve:

☐ Personal knowledge that you are doing a good job.

☐ Wage/salary increase.

☐ No anxiety about performance evaluations.

☐ Fewer customer complaints.

☐ Feeling of being a "professional."

☐ Respect/esteem from customers, peers, and your boss.

☐ Knowledge that your job is secure.

☐ Better relationship with your manager.

☐ Job enjoyment.

☐ Promotion.

☐ Freedom from on-the-job accidents.

☐ Increase in tips (where applicable).

☐ Freedom from on-the-job boredom.

☐ Less tiresome work.

☐ Participation in career development programs.

☐ Good first on-the-job experiences.

☐ Less stress.

☐ Improved teamwork.

☐ More fun on the job.

Guess what? Your employees will likely be happy with the same things that you checked. You may have checked all of the factors. Each is influenced by training.

WHEN CAN TRAINING HELP?

We've painted a bright picture of training. Done effectively, it's good for everyone–the manager, employees, and the customers. In other words, any organization will benefit from a good training program.

Will training solve all the problems of the business? Will all situations be improved by training?

The answer to both questions is "*No.*"

WHEN WILL TRAINING HELP?

Training will only help resolve problems when employees want to learn (have the proper attitude) and when job knowledge is lacking or inadequate. When these two factors are not present, other management solutions are more appropriate.

WHEN WILL TRAINING WORK?

Imagine a situation in which the manager thinks about the affected employee in terms of perceived attitude ("good" or "poor") and level of job knowledge ("high" or "low").

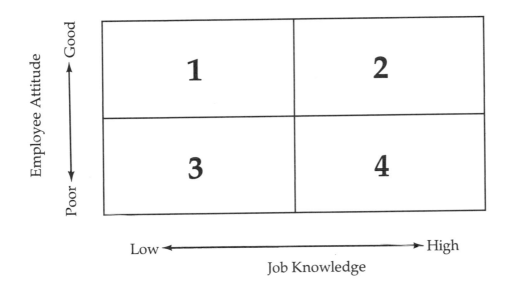

Let's look at each of the possibilities:

BOX 1 (Good Attitude/Low Job Knowledge)—An employee with a good attitude and low level of job knowledge *can* be helped dramatically by training.

BOX 2 (Good Attitude/High Job Knowledge)—In this situation training will help providing there is adequate time, etc.

BOX 3 (Poor Attitude/Low Job Knowledge)—In this situation personnel action (such as reassigning duties) may be most appropriate. Training is unlikely to help if the person who needs training is not interested in learning.

BOX 4 (Poor Attitude/High Job Knowledge)—This employee could do the job with the proper attitude, but without it, training will not reduce the problem.

Training works when the employee wants to learn (has a positive attitude) but does not know how to do required work.

WHAT TRAINING ISN'T!

So–training doesn't work in every situation. It works best for employees who are interested in learning the knowledge and skills required to do the job.

WHAT DO EMPLOYEES GET OUT OF TRAINING?

TAKE THE TRAINING TEST

Which of the following statements about training are True? False? or Partially True? (Maybe?) Check your answers and compare them to the author's statements below.

		True	False	Maybe
1.	Training can be difficult.	☐	☐	☐
2.	Training should be cost-effective.	☐	☐	☐
3.	Training is a line responsibility.	☐	☐	☐
4.	Only new employees benefit from training.	☐	☐	☐
5.	Training can modify an employee's attitudes.	☐	☐	☐
6.	Training is best when objectives involve increasing/changing, knowledge/skill levels.	☐	☐	☐
7.	Training should be done when time permits.	☐	☐	☐
8.	Training for problem resolution is different than teaching a new employee job skills.	☐	☐	☐

Check your answers.

1. True—Training can be difficult; it takes skillful planning to implement a quality training program.
2. True—Training *must* be cost-effective or it should not be undertaken.
3. True—Line Managers—not those in the personnel office—should be ultimately responsible for training.
4. False—*All* employees benefit from training.
5/6. Maybe—It is difficult to modify attitudes. Training is most typically helpful in influencing knowledge/skill levels.
7. False—Training is too important to do only when time permits; it must receive a priority.
8. False—The basic training techniques are the same regardless of the purpose.

LEARN THE TRAINING BASICS; THEY ALWAYS WORK

This guide will present the basics of training. These basics should be used consistently:

–To train (orient) new employees

–To upgrade the knowledge/skills of existing staff

–To provide long-term professional development

–To resolve operating problems

Once the basics of training are mastered they can be used any time training activities are being utilized.

Training should *not* be difficult for those who complete this book. Readers will learn how to define jobs and acquire the knowledge and skills necessary to be a good trainer.

Are you concerned about the answer to question #1 on the Training Test (page 11: Training can be difficult)? We answered this question "yes" because training *is* difficult for many persons. It takes a special effort to define *how* jobs should be done and to plan the subsequent training. It is also difficult because a trainer must have knowledge and skills which go beyond "common sense" and on-the-job experience.

TRAINING BASICS ARE UNIVERSAL

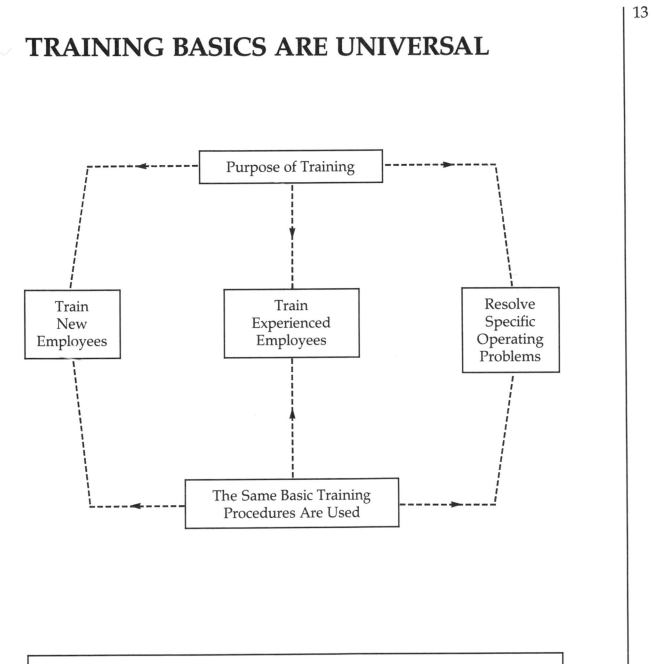

The basic procedures for effective training (regardless of the depth of the training) involves a four-step method. This method is the basis for much of the remainder of this book.

THE FOUR STEPS OF TRAINING

Regardless of the purpose of the training program (to teach new employees to upgrade knowledge/skills of experienced employees, or to resolve operating problems); or the type of training (individual or group) four basic steps are involved. They are:

Step #1–Define How the Job Should Be Done

Step #2–Plan the Training

Step #3–Present the Training

Step #4–Evaluate the Training

TRAINING IS LIKE PLAYING BASEBALL ⟩

Employees should not be trained to do a job until the *correct* way to do the work has been defined. This step is often omitted. Training activities need to be planned. Planning is often non-existent or inadequate. Professional trainers know that significant preparation is required *before* training begins.

TRAINING IS LIKE PLAYING BASEBALL

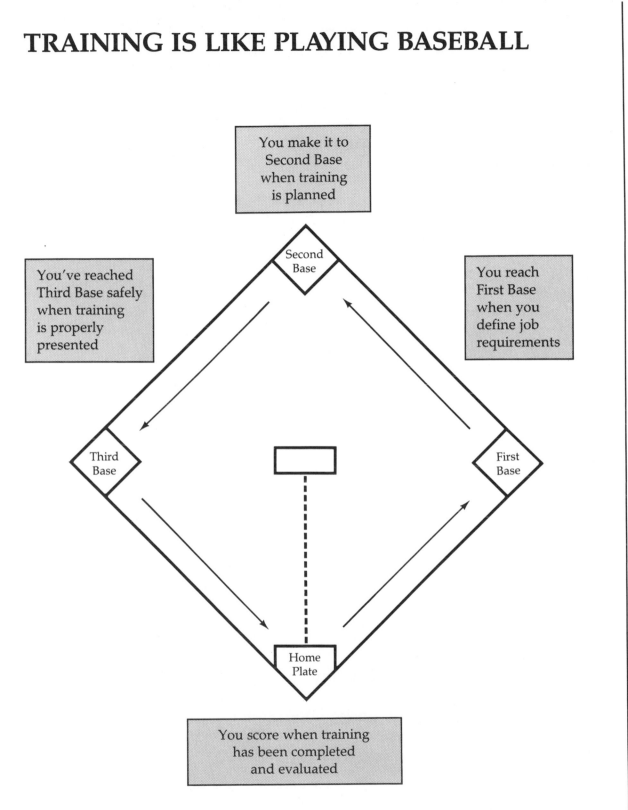

You make it to
Second Base
when training
is planned

You've reached
Third Base safely
when training
is properly
presented

You reach
First Base
when you
define job
requirements

Second
Base

Third
Base

First
Base

Home
Plate

You score when training
has been completed
and evaluated

THE FOUR STEPS OF TRAINING

STEP #1	DEFINE HOW THE JOB SHOULD BE DONE (POSITION ANALYSIS)

The first step in training is to define how the job you will train others for should be done. This process involves developing a position analysis.

> A Trainer must know how the job should be done before the "best" way can be taught.

The following activities are required to develop a position analysis:

■ Develop a List of Tasks   (Definition: Task–a single element/activity of a job. Jobs typically are composed of several different specific tasks.)

■ Define the Task   (Definition: A description of *exactly* how a task should be performed.)

■ Determine the Required Quality Level for each task

■ Construct a Job Description

A trainer knows that a position analysis is an important first step in training. He/she also knows, however, that the process used must be simple, practical, and efficient.

WHY A POSITION ANALYSIS?

Check (☑) each of the following statements as they apply to your organization.

T   F

☐ ☐   1. All employees in the same position perform each task of their job in the same way.

☐ ☐   2. Every supervisor for a specific area of responsibility would give the same explanation of how each task should be done.

☐ ☐   3. It takes different employees approximately the same amount of time to perform a specific task.

☐ ☐   4. All employees use the same process/procedures to perform identical tasks.

☐ ☐   5. Customers compliment your organization about the consistency of employee task procedures they encounter.

☐ ☐   6. Similar quality standards are consistently attained by all employees.

☐ ☐   7. The definition of what constitutes ''good'' performance is understood by all members of the staff and is used as the basis for training, supervision, and performance appraisals.

☐ ☐   8. Job descriptions accurately portray the work to be done.

If you answered honestly, it is probable you answered all statements false. If you think about each question, however, you probably recognize that in an *ideal* organization, most questions could be answered true.

When job tasks are performed with consistency by employees, quality standards can be defined; time and cost requirements can be established; and guidelines for performance evaluation criteria can be developed.

TRAINING: STEP #1 (Continued)

Position Analysis: The Four Activities
☑ Develop a List of Tasks
☐ Define a Task
☐ Determine Required Quality Levels
☐ Design a Job Description

ACTIVITY #1:
DEVELOP A LIST OF TASKS

The first activity for a quality Position Analysis is the development of a task list. This "list" will specify all job elements which a person (such as a sales clerk, computer operator, or maintenance supervisor) must do to satisfy the job requirements of that position. Once a manager/ trainer identifies and lists these activities, the parameters of a training program will have been defined.

How is a task list developed?

- Think about the required tasks to perform a specific job.

- Observe employees in that job. Observe what they do.

- Discuss with employees the tasks they do and ask their opinions about which are the most important and why.

- Ask other supervisors to identify tasks which their subordinates perform in similar job situations.

- Study the job description to see how accurately it reflects the objectives of the specific job.

SAMPLE TASK LIST

Position: _____

Tasks required to perform in this position, (listed by priority):

1. _____

2. _____

3. _____

4. _____

5. _____

6. _____

All significant tasks which an employee working in a specific position must do should be listed. For example, a sales clerk may, as part of the job:

—operate the cash register correctly for each transaction (daily)

—complete a daily sales report to the specifications required (daily)

—attend to the needs of customers (daily)

—conduct inventory counts (weekly)

—vacuum the carpet (daily)

—etc.

Once all basic tasks have been identified, a person with training responsibilities will know what a *new* sales clerk must accomplish.

To be successful, a training program must present all of the necessary information to allow a recently hired sales clerk to understand and perform the job to the level of quality expected.

Want to try an experiment to learn more about Task Lists? See page 69 to apply what you have learned.

TRAINING: STEP #1 (Continued)

Position Analysis: The Four Activities
☐ Develop a List of Tasks
☑ Define a Task
☐ Determine Required Quality Levels
☐ Design a Job Description

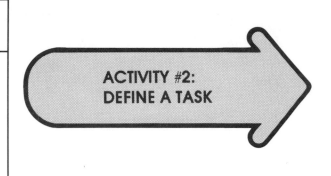

ACTIVITY #2:
DEFINE A TASK

The second activity to develop a Position Analysis is to design a method to "break down" each task. This breakdown answers the question, "How *exactly* should a task be performed?" It should tell the "how, when, and what" of each task and specify any required equipment, supplies, or procedures that are needed.

How is a task breakdown developed? Basically, the same process used to develop a task list can be employed, i.e.:

- A manager/trainer should think about the preferred way to perform a task.

- Employees who do the work should be observed and consulted.

- Supervisors of those who do similar tasks should be asked to explain how to ideally complete each task.

> NOTE: It is likely that a careful analysis of how work is currently done will yield excellent ideas about how it can be improved. While a "new way" is not always better, there are often better ways to accomplish any task.

SAMPLE TASK BREAKDOWN

Position: _____   Task _____

The procedures to complete this task include:

Step	Process	Equipment/ Supplies	Time Requirements	Other
1.				
2.				
3.				
4.				
5.				

A task breakdown describes, in sequence, what employees must do in order to perform a task correctly. Consider, for example, a sales clerk operating a cash register. Operating instructions provided by the manufacturer of the equipment might be an excellent starting point. These can then be integrated into the specific job requirements.

Or, how exactly should inventory counts be taken? What considerations are necessary when approaching a customer, etc.? The answers to these questions cannot be supplied in a manufacturer's instruction booklet. The procedures which evolve to answer questions such as these can be very beneficial *even before training activities begin!*

Want to try an experiment to learn more about
Task Breakdowns? See page 70 in the back of this book.

TRAINING: STEP #1 (Continued)

Position Analysis: The Four Activities
☐ Develop a List of Tasks
☐ Define a Task
☑ Determine Required   Quality Levels
☐ Design a Job Description

ACTIVITY #3:
DETERMINE REQUIRED
QUALITY LEVELS

The third activity in Position Analysis is the consideration of the quality level required for the task. What must be done to assure these quality standards are met? These are the questions this activity in the position analysis process addresses.

Today everyone is talking about the need for improved quality. Studies show that customers are willing to pay extra for quality service. On the other hand businesses lose customers when quality is lacking. Customers have long memories when quality problems occur.

Managers must design quality standards into the way work is done. The training program must stress quality and more importantly show each employer why it is essential.

Trainers must:

– Assure that the task breakdown, will yield output that meets or exceeds quality standards.

– Constantly stress quality as an integral part of each task.

– Show how quality standards are built into work output.

– Indentify those products/services which do not meet quality standards and correct them.

NOTE: Trainees may *not* be able to attain required quality levels immediately. Time is needed to build skills necessary to meet quality standards. Employees should be able to identify quality requirements by the time training is completed however, and understand by when the desired quality levels need to be met.

QUALITY STANDARDS TEST

Check (☑) the following statements which are true in your organization:

☐ 1. Quality standards have been established for all activities undertaken by persons in all positions.

☐ 2. Quality of work output is a significant factor in employee appraisals.

☐ 3. Customer complaints about quality problems are *extremely* rare.

☐ 4. Quality is just as important as quantity when tasks are performed.

☐ 5. Quality standards are consistently measured and reported on.

☐ 6. Management's philosophy and expectations about maintaining quality standards are well known.

☐ 7. Employee training programs emphasize quality requirements as skills that are taught.

☐ 8. Employees are rewarded by meeting (exceeding) quality goals.

How many did you check as true? Any that were not checked true need immediate attention.

Think about the products and services you purchase as a consumer. What makes you happy? Disappointed? What factors in your personal situation are applicable to the products/services provided by your organization? What can you learn from this analysis? How can you apply your own perceptions of quality to "the way things are done" by your employees?

TRAINING: STEP #1 (Continued)

Position Analysis:
The Four Activities
☐ Develop a List of Tasks
☐ Define a Task
☐ Determine Required Quality Levels
☑ Design a Job Description

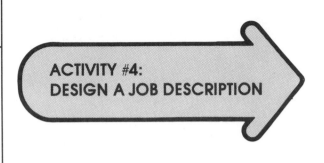

ACTIVITY #4:
DESIGN A JOB DESCRIPTION

The final activity in the Position Analysis process is to develop a job description. This important personnel management tool has many uses. A trainer with a current job description has a "head start" to assure that employees recruited and selected have the "right" training activities.

NOTE: Large organizations typically have personnel departments to help recruit employees. It is very important that operating departments provide the personnel department with updated job descriptions. If this does not occur, there may be "surprises" when a newly hired employee "discovers" what the job really involves.

SAMPLE JOB DESCRIPTION*

Position: _____ Date of Last Revision: ___/___/___

Level: _____

1. This position reports to: _____

2. This position supervises: _____

3. Basic tasks for this position include:

   A. _____

   B. _____

   C. _____

   D. _____

   E. _____

   F. _____

   G. _____

   H. _____

4. Knowledge of equipment required includes:

   _____

5. Personal qualifications judged most important for this job are:

   _____

6. Quality standards for this position assure:

   _____

7. Description of other important aspects of this position are:

   _____

8. Etc.

   _____

—Only the most important tasks should be included in the job description.

—"Personal qualities" are sometimes included in a separate "Job Specifications" sheet. We have combined them here.

*Note: This is a simplified version of a job description.

USES OF A JOB DESCRIPTION

Once developed, a job description can be used for many purposes, a few include:

- –To inform applicants being recruited about important aspects of the job.

- –To indicate the parameters of job requirements to be addressed during training.

- –As a management tool to help supervise employees.

- –To assist in employee appraisal (employees should be evaluated based on how well they do the work described in the job description).

Job descriptions are useful *after* an employee has been hired, as well as when applicants are being recruited. *

GET "HANDS ON" EXPERIENCE WITH A
JOB DESCRIPTION

_____

*For two excellent books where more can be learned about job descriptions, ordering *PERSONAL PERFORMANCE CONTRACTS* and *EFFECTIVE PERFORMANCE APPRAISALS* using the information in the back of the book.

MORE ABOUT JOB DESCRIPTION

Respond to the following questions. (Suggested answers are at the bottom of the page.)

1. How do job descriptions relate to training programs?

_____

_____

_____

2. What can happen if job descriptions are not current?

_____

_____

_____

3. What is the difference between a job description and a performance appraisal.

_____

_____

Want more experience with Job Descriptions?
See page 71 in the back of this guide.

Answers:

1. Job descriptions specify tasks for which training is necessary. They also help assure that qualified employees are hired.

2. Problems will occur when job descriptions do not accurately describe the work that needs to be done.

3. Job descriptions describe tasks which are part of a position. Performance appraisals are methods used by management to evaluate how well a job is being performed.

THE FOUR STEPS OF TRAINING (Continued)

STEP #2 **PLAN THE TRAINING**

We have now learned the importance of developing a position analysis. As a result, a manager/trainer should know all major aspects of the job that need to be done. Training based on the position analysis must (a) address all tasks, (b) teach the correct procedures, and (c) determine the required quality levels.

The second step in training is planning. Some individuals omit or de-emphasize this step (What is there to plan? We do the work every day and should be able to show someone how to do it. Time saved in planning can be spent in training!). *Failure to plan for training activities is a sure way to have your training efforts fail!*

To plan for training, a trainer must:

-Consider Training Objectives

-Develop a Training Plan

-Design a Training Lesson

-Select the Trainee(s)

-Prepare the Trainee(s)

HOW NOT TO PLAN

WHY PROPER PLANNING IS REQUIRED

Think about training programs in which you've been involved. Some may be currently used in your organization. Did any of the following occur? (If so, check the box ☑.)

☐ 1. The trainer "forgot" that training was to take place.

☐ 2. As a trainee, you were uncertain about what you needed to learn.

☐ 3. The training was often interrupted because of outside priorities.

☐ 4. The quality of training was lowered by the lack of supplies or unavailable equipment.

☐ 5. The procedures taught by the trainer were not consistent with:

    ☐ what the written or audio/visual materials said to do

    ☐ what others told you to do

    ☐ what you *saw* others do

☐ 6. The training was unorganized, (for example, procedures were taught out of sequence).

☐ 7. The trainer did not seem to care about training you.

☐ 8. The trainer was ineffective because of attitude or a lack of knowledge.

☐ 9. There were no written (or other) materials to help you learn.

☐ 10. Training was done "only when there was time."

If you had first-hand experience with any of the above items, *you now know why training is important!*

TRAINING: STEP #2 (Continued)

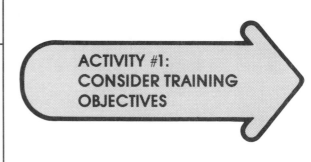

Planning for Training:
☑ Consider Training Objectives
☐ Develop a Training Plan
☐ Design a Training Lesson
☐ Select the Trainer(s)
☐ Prepare the Trainer(s)

**ACTIVITY #1:
CONSIDER TRAINING
OBJECTIVES**

The first concern when planning is to consider the training objectives.

> You can't plan a program until you first know what the training is to accomplish.

Recall at the beginning of this book we stated some objectives. These were stated in terms of what you (the reader) should know or be able to do after you complete this guide. As the trainer, when you plan a training program, it is equally important to consider what the trainees should know or be able to do after the training is completed.

Training objectives should be attainable. Both trainer and trainees will be frustrated if impossible-to-reach goals are set. Objectives should also be measureable. At the conclusion of training, the trainer and trainees should be able to tell how well the goals were met.

Objectives help during the evaluation stage which will be discussed later. The training program will be successful if the objectives are met.

TRAINING OBJECTIVES MUST BE ATTAINABLE *AND* MEASURABLE

Which of the following training programs objectives are attainable and measurable?

	Attainable	Measurable
1. There will never be any accidents.	☐	☐
2. Accident rates can be reduced.	☐	☐
3. Employees will always have the proper attitude about safety.	☐	☐
4. Employees can be taught to operate the equipment according to procedures in the task breakdown.	☐	☐
5. Employees will appreciate the need to operate equipment safely.	☐	☐
6. Employees can be trained to correctly complete an accident follow-up report.	☐	☐
7. Employees can be trained to correctly perform each task for their position.	☐	☐

Check your answers here:

1. This probably not attainable but is measurable. Accidents can be reduced but not eliminated (due to the human factor).

2. This is probably attainable and can be measured by determining if the rate after training is lower than before training.

3. Attitudes are difficult to "measure," this is probably not an attainable objective.

4. This is attainable and measurable.

5. Same answer as #3.

6. This is attainable and measurable. The definition of "correctly" refers to procedures outlined in the job breakdown for each task.

7. Both attainable and measurable.

TRAINING: STEP #2 (Continued)

Planning for Training:
☐ Consider Training Objectives
☑ Develop a Training Plan
☐ Design a Training Lesson
☐ Select the Trainer(s)
☐ Prepare the Trainer(s)

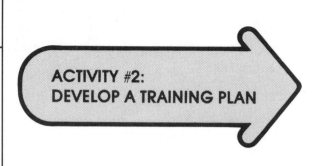

ACTIVITY #2:
DEVELOP A TRAINING PLAN

Once attainable and measurable training objectives have been considered, a training plan can be developed. This planning tool provides a step-by-step written document for others to follow.

A training plan can be for either a *complete* training program or something focusing on just one task.

SAMPLE TRAINING PLAN

Session	Date	Time	Employees Involved	Training Objective	Training Site	Trainer(s)	Equipment or Supplies	Method/ Lesson #
1	6/8	8:00 - 10:00	JH/JS	1, 2	Lunchroom	Jim	OH proj.	Lecture 1
2	6/15	9:00 - 10:00	JH/JS	3, 4	Sales Office	Jim	VHS/mon.	Individual 2
3	6/22	7:30 - 9:30	JH/JS	5, 6	Sales Office	Jim	Blackboard	Lecture 3
4	etc.							
10	8/12	10:00 - 11:00	JH/JS	19, 20	Client's Office	Jim	None	Individual 10

NOTE: Training plans outline a broad schedule. General plans are normally designed for several sessions. See page 72 for a ''hands on'' opportunity to work with a training plan.

TRAINING: STEP #2 (Continued)

Planning for Training:

☐ Consider Training Objectives

☐ Develop a Training Plan

☑ Design a Training Lesson

☐ Select the Trainer(s)

☐ Prepare the Trainer(s)

ACTIVITY #3:
DESIGN A TRAINING LESSON

Once a training plan outlining general program requirements has been developed, a trainer will need to concentrate on specific segments of that plan. This is done with the use of a training lesson. Generally, there is one training lesson for each training session. (If 10 sessions are planned, 10 training lessons are developed.)

A training lesson does several things. It:

- provides a content outline for the session
- suggests activities/specific instructions which will help facilitate training
- defines suggested time to be spent on each segment within the session

---

TASK BREAKDOWNS ARE USED FOR TRAINING LESSONS

If the specific training session is designed to teach employees how to perform a task, the task breakdown becomes a major part of the training lesson. An important job planning tool becomes an important training tool!

TRAINING LESSONS ORGANIZE TRAINING SESSIONS

What *exactly* does the trainer do during a training session? How much time should be allowed? These are questions answered by a training lesson. Consider the sample below:

SAMPLE TRAINING LESSON

Training Topic: _____ Operate company cash register properly _____

Objective(s): _____ Once training is completed, a sales clerk should know how to operate the cash register to company specifications. _____

Content of Session	Suggested Activities	Time
1. Procedures for cash register operations are found in the operations manual for the machine and augmented by company manuals for special purchases.	1. Provide a copy of instructions from the manual.	N/A
	2. Talk through the operating techniques.	10 min.
	3. Use training software, work through several examples of machine operation.	40 min.
	4. Review what has been learned by allowing trainees to demonstrate understanding via "real world" examples.	10 min. per trainee

NOTE: The content column may include actual information (such as the task breakdown) or information the instructor has adapted from other resources such as books or magazines. Suggested activities should allow trainees to participate in the training program.

For a "hands on" experience developing a training lesson see page 73.

TRAINING: STEP #2 (Continued)

Planning for Training:

☐ Consider Training Objectives

☐ Develop a Training Plan

☐ Design a Training Lesson

☑ Select the Trainer(s)

☑ Prepare the Trainer(s)

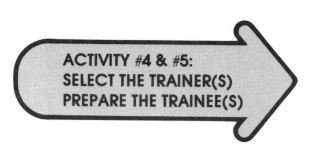

ACTIVITY #4 & #5:
SELECT THE TRAINER(S)
PREPARE THE TRAINEE(S)

Who is going to train? What should the trainer do to get the trainees ready for the training?

Training is one of the most important things any organization does. We have discussed how to plan for training. This concern must carry through to the trainer. When a busy supervisor or employee is asked to provide on-the-job training to a new staff member but is not given release time nor is told how to train, problems will result.

WHAT ABOUT PREPARING TRAINEES?

Trainees must be considered. They must be prepared for the experience. To prepare trainees, consider ways to:

–Reduce anxieties by telling trainees what the training will involve.

–Emphasize that trainee concerns will be addressed.

–Inform trainees that training will directly relate to the work they were hired to do.

–Indicate that efforts will be made to keep the training experience enjoyable and worthwhile.

–Let trainees know the basis on which they will be evaluated.

WHO WILL BE A GOOD TRAINER?

Not everyone will be an effective trainer. Which of the following characteristics/factors do you think are important to consider when selecting a trainer? (Check ☑ those which you think are important, then compare your beliefs with those of the author below.)

☐ 1. The best trainers will be found in the Personnel Department.

☐ 2. The most experienced employee will automatically be the best trainer.

☐ 3. The trainer must have an interest in training.

☐ 4. The trainer should have a sense of humor.

☐ 5. The trainer must be a good communicator.

☐ 6. The trainer must have patience.

☐ 7. The trainer must be a manager.

☐ 8. The trainer must have the time to train.

☐ 9. The trainer must have the respect of colleagues.

☐ 10. The trainer must be "higher up" in the organization.

☐ 11. The trainer must be enthusiastic.

☐ 12. The trainer must be the person who developed the training plan and training lesson.

☐ 13. The trainer must personally know how to do every task that is required of someone in the position being trained.

The following characteristics are important in a trainer:

3, 4, 5, 6, 8, 9, 11

NOTE: #13 is incorrect because different trainers could be used to teach employees different tasks.

THE FOUR STEPS OF TRAINING (Continued)

| STEP #3 | PRESENT THE TRAINING: GROUP OR INDIVIDUAL |

The third step in the training process becomes important once work procedures have been defined and *after* the training is planned. The training must be presented to the trainee(s).

No doubt, the decision to use group or individual methods was addressed as the training was planned.

There are a wide range of useful training methods. These include:

    – *Lectures* – where a trainer talks to the trainees. Videos, overheads, slides, films, etc. can supplement the lecture.

    – *Role-playing* – trainees act out situations after learning basic principles

    – *Case Studies* – trainees read, analyze, and discuss real life situations

    – *Demonstration* – a trainer (or other party) shows how to do something

    – *Self-Study Materials* – (Such as this book)

These can be used for both groups and individual training. There are also other types of individual training. However, the most common method–and that which will be reviewed at length in this book–is on-the-job-training (OJT).

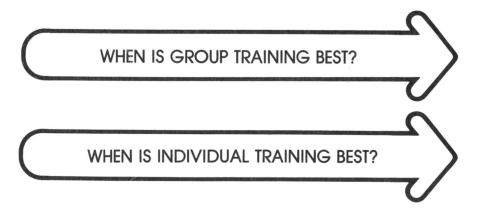

WHEN IS GROUP TRAINING BEST?

WHEN IS INDIVIDUAL TRAINING BEST?

GROUP OR INDIVIDUAL TRAINING: WHICH SHOULD BE USED WHEN?

What factors should be considered when deciding which type of training—group or individual—to use? Compare your beliefs with those of the author at the bottom of the page. (Check ☑ the type of training which is generally best for each factor.)

	Best Training Method	
Situation	**Group**	**Individual**
1. The same information needs to be presented to several persons.	☐	☐
2. The primary purpose of training is to present a wide range of extensive details.	☐	☐
3. When time is limited and several trainees must be trained.	☐	☐
4. When trainees' experience and background are similar.	☐	☐
5. When cost is a consideration.	☐	☐
6. When training needs to personally involve the trainee.	☐	☐
7. When highly specialized training is required.	☐	☐
8. Training that requires the least amount of training.	☐	☐

Answers:

Group training	Individual training
1, 3, 4, 5	2, 6, 7

#8—neither, both methods require extensive planning.

TRAINING: STEP #3 (Continued)

GROUP TRAINING: SOME IMPORTANT PRINCIPLES

Regardless of the group training method selected, some important principles should be addressed before the program is planned and implemented.

These principles center around the need for a trainer to practice the "art and science" of training.

Concepts useful in group training can be categorized as:

- –planning principles

- –implementing principles

- –evaluating principles

TAKE THE GROUP TRAINING TEST: What factors help assure training success?

NOTE: Most successful training programs utilize both group and individual activities. Regardless of the type of program, the principles are the same. Training cannot be successful if the basic principles shown above are not incorporated into the program.

WHICH OF THESE FACTORS ARE TRUE ABOUT GROUP TRAINING?

Check ☑ each of the following statements as either true or false. Compare your answers with those of the author below.

	True	False
1. Group training programs do not require a statement of objectives because each trainee is likely to finish training at a different skill level.	☐	☐
2. The results of group training should be evaluated when the training is completed as well as after when trainees return to the job.	☐	☐
3. Rehearsals of group training activities are unnecessary. Spontaneous presentations are best.	☐	☐
4. Training presentations are important but the training environment is not.	☐	☐
5. If handout materials are used, it is unnecessary for a trainer to provide an oral overview of the program when it begins.	☐	☐
6. If training is being conducted to resolve a problem, both the problem and the results of the solution should be discussed beforehand.	☐	☐
7. Participants in group training are more unlikely to resist change than those given individual training.	☐	☐
8. If a trainer is effective, each participant in the group training is likely to react the same way during training.	☐	☐
9. Good trainers will adapt their style to the needs of the group.	☐	☐
10. It is generally unwise to ask questions of trainees unless a trainer is concerned about "filling" time.	☐	☐

Answers:

The answers to questions #2, #6, and #9 are true; all other answers are false.

TRAINING: STEP #3 (Continued)

ON-THE-JOB TRAINING

On-the-job training is the most popular training method in small organizations. It is a great method if done correctly. Many managers believe on-the-job training is the best method because (a) it is simple and fast, (b) no planning is required, and (c) it is a method anybody can use.

People who believe these things about on-the-job training are wrong! The method is great–but not for these reasons. On-the-job training *is* simple, but only if extensive planning has been done. It is not fast, because time for planning is necessary. The statement that "anybody can train" using this method is a myth. The same concerns about trainer selection and the need for pre-training preparation apply to on-the-job training as well as group training.

WHAT YOU SHOULD KNOW ABOUT
ON-THE-JOB TRAINING

Before discussing details of on-the-job training, it is important to understand that this method can only be effective when basic training principles are utilized. If they are not, training time will be wasted.

ON-THE-JOB TRAINING: WHAT YOU SHOULD KNOW

Before learning the details about on-the-job training there is some basic information you should know. *Each of the following statements about on-the-job training is true.* Check those you intend to incorporate in your training procedures.

☐ —Pre-planning is necessary. Task lists, task breakdowns, performance standards, training plans, and training lessons must be developed before on-the-job training can be used to train new employees.

☐ —Trainer selection is important. The trainer must want to train, have adequate job knowledge and understand and use basic training principles.

☐ —Written materials such as task breakdowns, operating procedure manuals, and handbooks can be helpful to reinforce what trainees learn.

☐ —Time for training must be provided. It is usually not adequate to simply allow a trainee to ''tag along'' with a more experienced employee as work is performed.

☐ —Before demonstrating a work task, it is essential to prepare the work area, collect all appropriate tools, supplies, and any other necessary items.

☐ —Evaluation is an integral part of on-the-job training. This should be considered as the program is planned. Some evaluation is necessary both as the program evolves and at the time of its completion.

☐ —Even if a supervisor delegates on-the-job training to a subordinate, it is important for the supervisor to ''keep up'' with training progress. This can be done by interviewing the trainer and trainee and closely observing the trainee as initial work activities are performed.

☐ —On-the-job training time should not be wasted teaching tasks an employee already understands. An initial study of the task list along with a demonstration of work required for some tasks can clear the way to emphasize activities with which the trainee is unfamiliar.

TRAINING: STEP #3 (Continued)

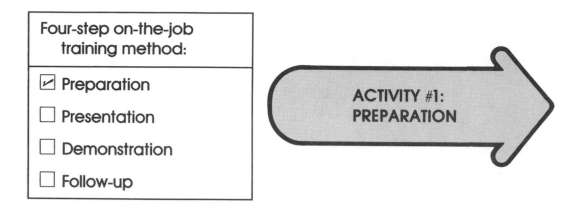

Four-step on-the-job
training method:

☑ Preparation

☐ Presentation

☐ Demonstration

☐ Follow-up

ACTIVITY #1:
PREPARATION

The first step in on-the-job training involves preparation. This step is the most important and, typically, the most overlooked. Simply stated, a trainer does not just "begin training." A wide range of activities must be done to help assure that training will be successful. Considering the impact that employees have on customers it is easy to justify careful planning.

We will discuss each step in on-the-job training on the facing page. This exercise will first identify an important training principle. Next, you will be asked to recall your personal experiences with on-the-job training programs. Finally, you will consider the negative implications that can arise if training principles are not incorporated.

Take time to complete these exercises carefully. After completing the work sheet you will have a greater knowledge about the "mechanics" of developing, implementing, and evaluating an on-the-job training program.

ON-THE-JOB TRAINING: PREPARATION

Complete the following exercise. In Column 1 indicate whether the factor noted was addressed in the last on-the-job training program you attended. In Column 2 think about the problem(s), if any, that can occur if the factor is not used.

Training Concept/Factor	True In Your Most Recent On-The-Job Training?		Problem(s) if not used
	Yes	No	
1. Before training began you knew what you were to learn and how long the training would last.			
2. A written task breakdown was used.			
3. The work area was ready and all equipment supplies were present before training began.			
4. You were made comfortable before the training began. There was little stress, anxiety, or pressure in the training environment.			
5. You were given a chance to show you knew about selected tasks before training began, so you could learn only those activities with which you were unfamiliar.			
6. The trainer began each session by telling you what you were supposed to learn.			
7. The trainer had an effective way to evaluate whether you had learned each activity.			
8. You consistently observed "the right way" being used by other employees once the training session was completed.			

TRAINING: STEP #3 (Continued)

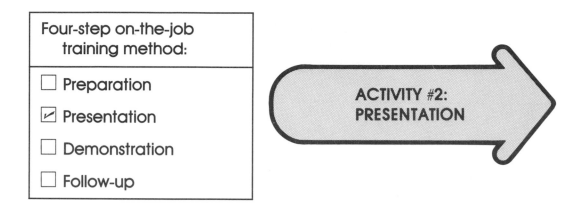

The second step in on-the-job training involves presentation to the trainee. This step should be easy if the trainer is prepared. This step is more than simply showing an employee how the work should be done. Rather, the trainer must have adequate time to explain to the trainee what must be done while carefully demonstrating the "whats and whys" of each procedure.

Many managers make the mistake of throwing a new employee into the new work setting without some initial training. They feel this technique hastens learning since the trainee will have to "do the work or else." This is usually not a good technique. Anxiety and stress can make the initial work experiences difficult for a new employee. Product quality and/or customer service can be affected. Your customers are not paying a reduced price when they are handled by a trainee. They should consistently receive the quality of the product/service which you promise. This cannot be done when a trainee learns "at the expense" of the customer. *Some training must be done before the trainee is put into a position where his or her output will reach the customer.*

ON-THE-JOB TRAINING: PRESENTATION

Complete the exercise below. In the first column indicate whether the training concept/factor was addressed in the last program you attended as a trainee. In Column 2 think about problem(s), if any, created if the factor is not used.

Training Concept/Factor	True In Your Most Recent On-The-Job Training?		Problem(s) if not used
	Yes	No	
1. Did the trainer explain each task to you before it was demonstrated?			
2. Did the trainer seem to enjoy and want to undertake the training?			
3. Did the trainer ask you questions and urge you to ask questions as the initial presentation evolved?			
4. Did each activity seem organized? Did it follow procedures written in a task breakdown?			
5. Did you receive the "right" amount of training in each session? (Could you have learned more or was too much "crammed" into the time interval?)			
6. Was the training you received accurate and simple?			
7. Was the training of interest to you? Were there things that the trainer could have done to make it more interesting?			
8. Could you tell that the trainer had done effective planning and had experience presenting this phase of the training program?			

TRAINING: STEP #3 (Continued)

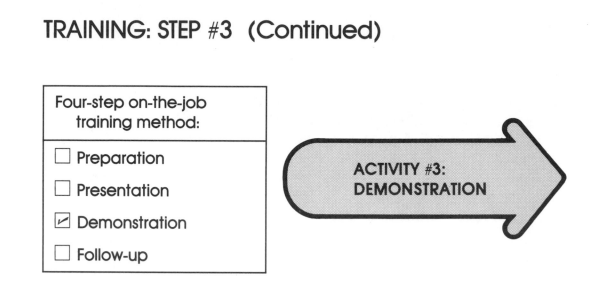

Four-step on-the-job training method:

- ☐ Preparation
- ☐ Presentation
- ☑ Demonstration
- ☐ Follow-up

ACTIVITY #3:
DEMONSTRATION

The third step in on-the-job training is demonstration. During this step the trainee should be allowed to show the trainer what has been learned. Done effectively, this step involves more than a trainer simply allowing the trainee to work alone and returning later to check performance. Rather, a trainer should closely observe the trainee and provide immediate feedback (positive reinforcement or corrective action help) to help the trainee apply what has been learned.

By now, you probably have noticed that the recommended approach to on-the-job training is different from those with which you have been involved. Can you see why the initial statements about the myths of on-the-job training (little time required, no preparation needed, "anyone" can train, etc.) are untrue? On-the-job training presents a powerful method to teach your employees what they need to know, but these results can only happen when the program is designed and implemented correctly.

ON-THE-JOB TRAINING: DEMONSTRATION

Complete the exercise below. In Column 1 indicate whether the factor noted in the training/concept factor was addressed in the last training program you attended. In Column 2 think about problem(s), if any, which can be created if the factor is not used.

Training Concept/Factor	True In Your Most Recent On-The-Job Training?		Problem(s) if not used
	Yes	No	
1. Did the trainer ask you to describe each activity as you initially performed it?			
2. Did the trainer have you demonstrate tasks?			
3. If you made errors, did the trainer promptly indicate what they were, explain exactly what was wrong and why it was wrong?			
4. If errors were made in your demonstration, did the trainer get upset and blame you for the error?			
5. If errors were made during your demonstration, did the trainer demonstrate the correct way and then allow you to practice the correct method?			
6. Did the trainer congratulate you when you did the work correctly?			
7. Did the trainer explain how the task you demonstrated was part of your training program?			
8. Did the trainer use a questioning process to help assess whether you knew why work was being done in a specified way?			
9. Did you have opportunities to demonstrate your learning in a situation which would not have a direct impact upon customers?			

TRAINING: STEP #3 (Continued)

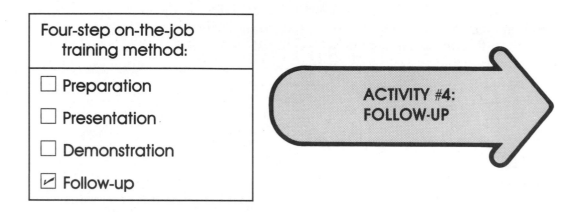

Four-step on-the-job training method:
☐ Preparation
☐ Presentation
☐ Demonstration
☑ Follow-up

ACTIVITY #4:
FOLLOW-UP

The final step in on-the-job training involves follow-up. Some managers and trainers omit this step. If the trainee has properly demonstrated the activity why is follow-up necessary? Over time, trainees forget the required work procedures. They may have "discovered shortcuts" that are not better methods than those presented during training. These are examples of when the trainer must, after observation, provide corrective action to "get trainees back on the track".

Follow-up involves evaluation. Is the trainee able to do the work in the correct manner? If the correct procedure is defined (a task breakdown is used for this purpose) and if the correct procedure is taught, the trainer should be able to confirm that training has been successful. Notice, however, if either of these steps is omitted (the "correct" method is not defined or taught) training will be ineffective and the fault will lie with the trainer–not the trainee.

ON-THE-JOB TRAINING: FOLLOW-UP

Complete the exercise below. In Column 1 indicate whether the training concept/factor was addressed in the last training program you attended. In Column 2 think about the problem(s), if any, which can be created if the factor is not used.

Training Concept/Factor	True In Your Most Recent On-The-Job Training?		Problem(s) if not used
	Yes	No	
1. Did the trainer provide any follow-up evaluation?			
2. Did the trainer encourage you to ask questions after the training was completed?			
3. Did you know who to ask for follow-up help, if any was needed?			
4. Did the trainer/manager conduct follow-up observations of your work?			
5. Were you provided with encouragement when observations indicated the work was being done correctly?			
6. Were you asked for ideas about how the job might be improved?			
7. Were you asked about ways the training program might be improved?			
8. Did you feel "good" about the training experience?			
9. Was the training experience related to the work you did immediately after training?			
10. Would more or different training have been more effective?			

THE FOUR STEPS OF TRAINING (Continued)

STEP #4   **TRAINING EVALUATION: BACK TO THE OBJECTIVES**

We have indicated that there are four steps involved in training:

STEP #1:   Define the job (Position Analysis)

STEP #2:   Plan the training: Think about objectives

STEP #3:   Present the training: Group or individual

STEP #4:   Evaluate the training (Think about the objectives)

We have reached the point to discuss Step #4 (Evaluation). The need for this step has already been emphasized; our job is now to reinforce how important it is.

Why Evaluate? All trainers need to learn if their training has been successful. If it has, the subject matter, approach, and method may be used for additional training efforts. If it has not, current trainees may need additional training and future programs may need to include different subject matter and/or utilize different training methods or techniques.

PRINCIPLES OF TRAINING EVALUATION

> The list below indicates some important concepts of training evaluation. Check those concepts you use in your training programs. Carefully consider the other concepts, they may help you more effectively evaluate the worth of your training efforts.

☐ 1. Evaluation efforts must address the extent to which *measurable* objectives stated at the beginning of the training are attained.

☐ 2. Evaluation must focus on:
  - ☐ training methods
  - ☐ training content
  - ☐ training environment

☐ 3. Trainees can be *asked* about training experiences.

☐ 4. Trainees can be *observed* to assess training effectiveness.

☐ 5. Trainees can be *tested* to measure knowledge gained. (A *pretest* about subject matter can be given before the training begins; a *post-test* comprised of the same questions is given after training is completed.)

☐ 6. Trainers must realize that new techniques should be used if training evaluation consistently identifies problems.

☐ 7. Evaluation done before the conclusion of training can help a trainer identify areas where changes in training can be helpful.

☐ 8. As training programs are planned, trainers should consistently think about how they will be evaluated.

☐ 9. Trainers should use *results* of training evaluation to assess the cost effectiveness of training efforts.

TRAINING: STEP #4 (Continued)

COACHING: FOLLOW-UP IS CRITICAL

Is the training program completed once the evaluation has been done? The answer is NO! When does training stop and normal supervision begin? This question, while perhaps more one of language than substance, introduces us to the concept of coaching.

Coaching is the ongoing reinforcement of the positive aspects of training.   It involves:

   –focusing on special problems which must be resolved

   –maintaining open and effective communications with
     employees

   –providing employees with ongoing opportunities for professional
     growth

Coaching activities involve communicating with employees about work-related problems. Both the manager and the trainee will engage in a problem-solving process. Their relationship should improve, work should be done more effectively, and the customers should be better served.

GOOD COACHING SHOULD ALWAYS
BE FRIENDLY AND PRACTICAL

COACHING PRINCIPLES

Try to practice the following coaching principles during training sessions you conduct. Check ([✔]) the concepts you routinely use and make a serious effort to incorporate others into your future sessions.

☐   1.   Allow employees to become involved in the development of work procedures which they will use.

☐   2.   Permit employees to evaluate their work and make recommendations for improvement.

☐   3.   Undertake corrective action interviews in private.

☐   4.   Evaluate the work of each employee by comparing their performance against task breakdowns and job descriptions.

☐   5.   Focus on the procedures taught during training—and the way the trainee works on the job as the evaluation is done.

☐   6.   Establish time frames for corrective action.

☐   7.   Have the manager indicate his or her ideas about how work performance can be improved.

☐   8.   Establish a schedule for subsequent review of work performance.

☐   9.   Allow ample time for "trained" employees to develop skills and/or build speed.

☐   10.   Use open-ended questions to encourage each trainee to explain problems which they have encountered.

TRAINING: STEP #4 (Continued)

ORIENTATION: START OF TRAINING

A new applicant's first impressions about his or her job can make all the difference. The foundation for attitudes which may stay in place as long as that employee remains on the job are established during orientation.

SELECTION AND TURNOVER: A "CHICKEN AND EGG" PROBLEM?

Many organizations experience high levels of employee turnover. New employees are more likely to quit than long-term workers. What does it mean when there are high turnover levels? Were "bad" employee selection decisions made? Were "poor" employee management practices undertaken *after* the new employee began work? Are both factors common reasons for turnover? Regardless of whether the problem rests with selection, or supervision, or both, the result is the same. When an employee leaves, needless staffing expenses are incurred. Also service to customers is likely to decline. An employee's initial impressions of the company are important. Don't destroy all of the work done if bringing a "good" employee to the job by "turning off" that employee through improper orientation and poor training.

Orientation typically involves providing new employees with information that all employees, regardless of position, must know. The mission and objectives of the company. The policies and procedures that are applicable to all staff members. Where things are located, etc.

Orientation can be formal or informal, be done through discussion or the use of other media. Regardless of the methods used for orientation, these programs must be carefully planned to assure that new employees receive the information they need.

---

*For an excellent book on orientation, order *NEW EMPLOYEE ORIENTATION* using the information in the back of the book.

WHAT IS YOUR EXPERIENCE WITH ORIENTATION?

In many ways you are like the other employees joining your organization. You and your company may benefit from the following exercise. The attitudes you experienced during the orientation process are likely to be similar to those of other employees. The concerns, if any, which resulted from your orientation are likely to be repeated in others.

Carefully think about your initial experiences. Use this process to identify potential ways to improve your orientation program.

Yes No

☐ ☐ 1. I knew how long orientation would last.

☐ ☐ 2. I knew what the orientation process would involve.

☐ ☐ 3. My supervisor/trainer was prepared for orientation.

☐ ☐ 4. All of the questions and concerns I had as a new employee were answered during the orientation process.

☐ ☐ 5. I was encouraged to ask questions; and the answers resolved my concerns.

☐ ☐ 6. Following orientation I knew what training programs would be required and when they would be useful.

☐ ☐ 7. I felt ''good'' about my new organization as a result of the orientation program.

☐ ☐ 8. The peers I met during orientation were friendly and I was encouraged to get to know them.

☐ ☐ 9. During orientation I was provided with the necessary materials.

☐ ☐ 10. In retrospect, my orientation program was "good." It attained objectives designed to introduce new employees to the job.

ORIENTATION CHECKLIST

There are a wide range of policies, procedures, activities, and other concerns which should be addressed during the orientation process. How does a trainer/manager recall what these details are? What can be done to help assure all employees receive the same information? What can be done to help reduce the time necessary for pre-orientation planning?

An orientation checklist can be useful for these purposes. There are two basic ways an orientation checklist can be developed:

1. -Compile those points which must be addressed during orientation.

2. -Develop an employee handbook and distribute it at the time of orientation.

CAN YOU USE THIS ORIENTATION CHECKLIST?

A wide range of topics will probably be included in your orientation checklist. It is not possible to define each element for every organization. However, the list on the facing page may suggest topics that might be important for your organization. Consider each carefully. Delete those which are unnecessary and add others that would be helpful during your orientation efforts.

ORIENTATION CHECKLIST

Mark those topics you need to address in your orientation program. Make a check to indicate topics of importance. If applicable, share the marked list with your manager and then work to develop an improved orientation program which addresses all topics of special concern.

☐ Accidental Death Insurance
☐ Appearance and Dress
☐ Attendance
☐ Bulletin Boards
☐ Company Publications
☐ Dental Insurance
☐ Departmental Meetings
☐ Disciplinary System
☐ Educational Assistance
☐ Emergency Procedures
☐ Employee Opinion Survey
☐ Employee Recognition
☐ General Meetings
☐ Grievance Procedures
☐ Health, Safety, and Accident Policies
☐ Holidays
☐ Jury Duty Policies
☐ Layoff Policy
☐ Leaves of Absence
☐ Lost Articles
☐ Meals
☐ Medical and Life Insurance
☐ Name Badges
☐ Overtime
☐ Pay Advances

☐ Pay Discrepancies and Adjustments
☐ Pay Policy
☐ Paydays/Pay Periods
☐ Performance Appraisals
☐ Personal Property
☐ Probationary Period
☐ Recreational and Social Activities
☐ Retirement Program
☐ Seniority
☐ Service Awards Banquet
☐ Sick Leave
☐ Sign-In, Sign-Out Sheets
☐ Standards of Conduct
☐ Telephone Calls
☐ Time Records
☐ Tips
☐ Training Procedures
☐ Uniforms
☐ Vacations
☐ Wage & Salary Reviews
☐ Work Schedules
☐ Worker's Compensation Insurance
☐ Others
☐
☐

EMPLOYEES: DON'T FORGET THEIR ROLE IN TRAINING

Much of the information in this book has focused on the trainer. However, the trainer can never forget about the individuals for whom the program was developed.

With today's emphasis on quality service employees are becoming more involved in how a business operates. Many observers believe this trend will continue and trainees may well be involved in planning training programs that are most beneficial to them.

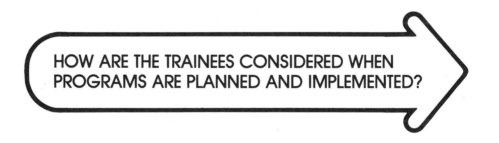

HOW ARE THE TRAINEES CONSIDERED WHEN PROGRAMS ARE PLANNED AND IMPLEMENTED?

There are many ways that trainees can be involved as programs are being planned and implemented. How many can you think of?

TRAINEES PLAY AN IMPORTANT ROLE IN TRAINING

Read the following list of ways to involve trainees as training programs are being developed. Check any procedures currently used in your training program. Also note those which are not currently used—but which should be.

In use	Not in use but needed	
☐	☐	Employees are surveyed about current training needs.
☐	☐	Employees are interviewed about ways that orientation programs can be improved.
☐	☐	Employees evaluate current training programs—and are given an opportunity to comment on how they can be improved.
☐	☐	Training programs maximize participation by trainees.
☐	☐	Trainees evaluate trainers following each program.
☐	☐	Trainees evaluate training environment following each program.
☐	☐	During performance reviews, employees are asked about the relationship between training activities and job requirements and performance.
☐	☐	Recent trainees are solicited to endorse the need for training with their peers.
☐	☐	Trainees are asked how to improve training during the program and not just at the conclusion of training.

TRAINING RESOURCES: HELP IS AVAILABLE

Trainers cannot simply sit at their desks to develop training programs. Even if they could, this is probably not the best way to spend valuable time. Fortunately there is a wide range of resource material that can be used when developing and conducting training activities.

Frequently, this information is available within the trainer's organization. If this is not the case, other resources should be used such as the public library, or in a local university, college, or technical training school.

A wise trainer will not wait until a program must be developed before applicable information is collected. Instead, resource material should be collected on an ongoing basis. Magazine articles, applicable brochures received through the mail, "interesting" brochures collected at trade shows, etc. Provide ideas where training resource materials can be found. The sources for excellent training materials are extensive.

SOURCES OF TRAINING MATERIALS

NOTE: Would you like additional information about resource materials? A brief list of training resource materials is provided on page 74. These magazines will provide additional information about training that can be helpful to you. Also, the self-study books described on page 75 have been extremely well received in the training programs of more than 12,000 organizations.

WHERE CAN I GO FOR HELP?

Check each of the training resources identified below which are available for your use. What must you do to begin developing a "library" of materials for all of your applicable training activities?

☐ Manufacturers' operating manuals (for equipment).

☐ A procedures manual for your organization.

☐ Task breakdowns for jobs within each department.

☐ Applicable magazines for your business.

☐ Applicable trade magazines devoted to training, human resource management, etc.

☐ Promotional flyers of training information from training companies.

☐ A list of training programs from nearby educational institutions.

☐ Libraries available to you.

☐ Membership information in applicable trade associations.

☐ Names and phone numbers of distributor's representatives selling products/equipment/supplies which can be useful during training.

☐ "Names and numbers of "friendly competition" (training ideas gained from those in related businesses).

☐ "Canned" training programs (packaged programs which present generic training information.

☐ Names of outside consultants who can be hired to teach specific programs to employees.

There are a wide range of resources available to help trainers develop programs. Make use of them whenever practical. Focus your efforts on delivering training programs—not developing them.

USING VISUAL AIDS

Nothing is worse than a boring lecture where there is no chance for trainees to become actively involved. Almost as bad is for a trainer to incorporate audio/visual effects into the training program and do it poorly.

Have you ever been in a situation where time was lost and an awkward scene evolved because a slide or film projector would not work, a videotape did not appear on the monitor, or a sound system didn't work?

Part of the preparation for any training activity must be a thorough orientation to any equipment which is to be used. Trainers must know how the equipment works and make sure that "back-up" equipment is available.

AVOID DATA DUMP

USING VISUAL AIDS: WHICH COMES FIRST?

You've heard the question many times: "Which came first, the chicken or the egg?" This question can, with revision, be asked as the trainer decides upon the role of visual aids in the training program: "Which comes first, training program content or visual aids?"

While we may debate about the first question (the chicken and egg), there can be no debate about the second: content must be determined before visual aids can be selected/developed. This may seem obvious, but many trainers make a mistake. For example, they may find an excellent videotape or a slide presentation dealing with a topic and *then* decide a training program involving this subject would be helpful. It is far better to decide the content first and then determine how that content should be presented.

While the use of a visual aid may be effective it is also possible that a "role play," handout, on-job demonstration, or other method might be better (and less expensive) than a visual aid.

Determine program content first and then find the best method to present it. Do not use a visual aid unless it is the "best" technique for delivering the training subject matter or clearly supports the content you are presenting.

A PAT ON THE BACK

None of the information presented in this book will be of use unless it is applied. Your challenge as you have worked through the book has been to consider how the material can be applied to the training activities with which you are involved. We hope this book has caused you to objectively consider ways to improve your training efforts.

The Certificate of Recognition on the facing page presents a tribute to your efforts. At the same time it suggests a simple pledge we hope you will make.

The job of a manager is very important. The training responsibilities which you assume as part of that position are significant. You directly affect the lives of your employees and the customers they serve. You have a significant influence on the future success of your organization. As a "prepared" trainer you will gain experiences that will help with your own professional growth.

Best of luck in all of your future training activities.

CONGRATULATIONS →

CERTIFICATE OF RECOGNITION

This is to certify that _____ has read and
(your name)
understood the basic information presented in *Training Managers*

To Train and promises to incorporate applicable methods and

procedures into future training activities as they are planned and

delivered. By so doing our future employees will become better

prepared to serve the organization.

Presented this date _____

by

_____
Your Manager or Trainer

"Back of the Guide"

The following pages contain additional activities which were designed to help you apply concepts presented earlier. All forms may be reproduced without further permission.

TASK LIST

You learned about task lists on page 19. To develop a task list, think about your job. Create a list on the form below for each task you do as part of your job responsibilities. *Be complete.* Ask others who do similar work to analyze your list for additions, deletions, changes. Ask your manager to do the same. You cannot develop a training program until all tasks for which training is necessary have been defined.

TASK LIST

Your position: _____

Tasks routinely performed in this position include:

1. _____
2. _____
3. _____
4. _____
5. _____
6. _____
7. _____
8. _____
9. _____
10. _____
11. _____
12. _____
13. _____
14. _____
15. _____

Use another sheet of paper if necessary.

TASK BREAKDOWN

You learned about task breakdowns on page 21. To develop a task breakdown select a task from your list on page 69. Use the form below to explain how it should be done. Share your task breakdown with others who do the same task. Is there agreement about the ''how, when, and what'' of the task? What problems arise when there is no agreement? What are the implications of any disagreement on the design and conduct of future training programs?

TASK BREAKDOWN			
Position: _____ Task: _____			
Step	Process	Equipment/Supplies	Other

Use additional paper to continue this analysis if necessary.

JOB DESCRIPTION

You learned about job descriptions on page 24. Complete the following form for your job. Show it to your boss. What differences, if any, exist in opinions about what your job involves? How can this affect *your* job performance?

JOB DESCRIPTION

Position: _____

Date of last revision: _____ / _____ / _____

1. I report to: _____

2. I supervise: _____

3. Basic tasks which are part of this position are: _____

    a. _____

    b. _____

    c. _____

    d. _____

    e. _____

    f. _____

    g. _____

    h. _____

4. Equipment which I use includes: _____
_____

5. Personal qualifications important for this job include: _____
_____

6. Other important aspects of this position are: _____
_____
_____

TRAINING PLAN

Use the format below to "sketch" a training program you are planning or that your organization conducts. (It may need to be modified to accommodate your specific requirements.)

Session #	Date	Time	Employees Scheduled	Training Objectives	Training Site	Trainer(s)	Equipment/ Supplies	Instructional Method

TRAINING LESSON

You learned about training lessons on page 35. Using the format below to develop a training lesson for one task that you regularly do as part of your job. (NOTE: You may wish to select the task for which you developed a task breakdown.)

Content of Session	Suggested Activities	Estimated Time Required

TRAINING LESSON

Training Topic: _____

Training Objective(s): _____

_____

ADDITIONAL TRAINING REFERENCES

If you want to learn more about training, check the following references for additional information:

Books

Zemke, R. and others. *Designing and Delivering Cost-Effective Training and Measuring the Results.* Minneapolis, Minnesota: Lakewood Publications, 1981.

Fournies, F. *Coaching for Improved Work Performance.* New York, New York: Van Nostrand Reinhold Co., 1978.

Mitchell, G. *The Trainer's Handbook: The AMA Guide to Effective Training.* New York, New York: AMACOM, 1987.

Eitington, J. *The Winning Trainer.* Houston, Texas: Gulf Publishing Co., 1984.

Newstrom, J. and Scannelly, E. *Games Trainers Play: Experiential Learning Exercises.* New York, New York: McGraw Hill Book Co., 1980.

Spaid, O. *The Consummate Trainer: A Practitioner's Perspective.* Englewood Cliffs, New Jersey: Prentice-Hall, 1986.

Ribler, R. *Training Development Guide.* Reston, Virginia: Reston Publishing Co., 1983.

Camp R. and others. *Toward a More Organizationally Effective Training Strategy and Practice.* Reston, Virginia: Reston Publishing Co., 1986.

Magazines

Training: The Magazine of Human Resources Development. Lakewood Publications (Lakewood Building, 50 South Ninth Street, Minneapolis, Minnesota 55402).

Trainer's Workshop. American Management Association (135 West 50th Street, New York, New York 10020).

NOTES

NOTES

NOTES

OVER 150 BOOKS AND 35 VIDEOS AVAILABLE IN THE 50-MINUTE SERIES

We hope you enjoyed this book. If so, we have good news for you. This title is part of the best-selling *50-MINUTE*™ *Series* of books. All *Series* books are similar in size and identical in price. Many are supported with training videos.

To order *50-MINUTE* Books and Videos or request a free catalog, contact your local distributor or Crisp Publications, Inc., 1200 Hamilton Court, Menlo Park, CA 94025. Our toll-free number is (800) 442-7477.

50-Minute Series Books and Videos Subject Areas . . .

Management
Training
Human Resources
Customer Service and Sales Training
Communications
Small Business and Financial Planning
Creativity
Personal Development
Wellness
Adult Literacy and Learning
Career, Retirement and Life Planning

Other titles available from Crisp Publications in these categories

Crisp Computer Series
The Crisp Small Business & Entrepreneurship Series
Quick Read Series
Management
Personal Development
Retirement Planning